Who Will You Be, Sweet Baby?

Tyler Whipple

AuthorHouse™
1663 Liberty Drive
Bloomington, IN 47403
www.authorhouse.com
Phone: 833-262-8899

This book is printed on acid-free paper.

ISBN: 978-1-6655-7100-5 (sc)
ISBN: 978-1-6655-7101-2 (e)

Print information available on the last page.

Published by AuthorHouse 09/16/2022

authorHOUSE®

This book is dedicated to my three children and inspired by the birth Zaylie Lynn. You can be whoever you want to be kids. I love you and I am so excited to see who you all become.

Love,
Dad

Who Will You Be, Sweet Baby?

Who will you be?

A vet,   a doctor,   a representative of
Tennessee?

Who will you be?

A nurse,  an engineer,  a sailor of the deep blue sea?

Who will you be?

Sweet baby, who will you be?

A policewoman, a machine operator, a taster of candy?

Who will you be?

A banker,  a teacher,  a lover of the finer things?

Who will you be?

Sweet baby, who will you be?

A cheerleader,   an artist,   a chaser of your
biggest dreams?

Who will you be?

A lover,   a fighter,   the sweetest thing
I've ever seen?

Who will you be?

Sweet baby, who will you be?

Momma's girl, daddy's world, we will love you, regardless, for eternity.

Printed in the United States
by Baker & Taylor Publisher Services